This notebook belongs to

____

Printed in Great Britain
by Amazon

34814285R10066